Depression:

Jesus is Calling You

A Christian Guide to Receiving Your Healing

P. A. Kennan

Onwards and Upwards Publishers

3 Radfords Turf, Cranbrook, Exeter,
Devon, EX5 7DX.
www.onwardsandupwards.org

ISBN: 978-1-78815-665-3
Typeface: Sabon LT
Illustration: Leah-Maarit
Graphic design: LM Graphic Design

Contents

In this world you will have trouble.
But take heart! I have overcome the world.

John 16:33

INTRODUCTION

Learn from Me

Come to me, all you who are weary and burdened, and I will give you rest. Take my yoke upon you and learn from me.

Matthew 11:28-29

I can vividly remember the first time the darkness descended upon me at the age of twelve. Of course, at that time I couldn't put a name to how I felt. In my twenties I learned what that name was: depression. I was at university, sitting in a lecture theatre, surrounded by hundreds of students. Suddenly, I lost all focus on what the lecturer was saying; he just faded away into the background. For absolutely no reason I started to cry and couldn't stop for days.

The student counsellor and my G.P. diagnosed depression and I found myself on antidepressants. Or, rather, I lost myself. The effects of the chemical cosh were worse than the depression. At least when I was depressed I knew who I was, where I was and what day it was! One day I flushed them down the loo, deciding that I was better off without them. And so life continued with occasional bouts. I put my depression down to it 'running in the family'; a close family member had committed suicide and another had attempted it. I thought it was just the way I was.

Then, in middle age, I got to a point where my first thought on waking was, "I'm still here; I don't want to be." One day my daughter came home from school early, unwittingly preventing me from taking an overdose. I felt deeply ashamed, appalled and horrified at what I'd been contemplating. By now I was a committed Christian and knew

5

that I should not be feeling this way. Christians don't get depressed. Do they? I came to the realisation that, just as the OCD that had dominated me from childhood had been overcome with God's help,[1] so this too needed to be faced up to and dealt with God's way.

This book is the result of that partnership – what I discovered as I tried to understand the roots of my depression so that it could be defeated. I found this to be an extremely challenging experience, requiring brutal honesty before God and with myself. But if you want to be well you have to change your thinking, and be prepared to face up to some uncomfortable truths.

The quote from Matthew 11:28-29 brings us the comfort and reassurance that we are not alone. Every time I read it, three words jump out: "learn from me". I've learned so much from reading Christ's words to us, and pray you will too. The 'world' – human wisdom; the way we all think and behave towards each other – brings us seemingly endless troubles and anxieties. Christ reassures us that he has overcome the world and we can too.

---

[1] For the full story, see P. A. Kennan, "OCD: Be Still and Know", (Leatherhead: Onwards and Upwards Publishers, 2015), ISBN 978-1-910197-66-0

CHAPTER ONE

What is Depression?

Why, my soul, are you downcast? Why so disturbed within me? Why must I go about mourning, oppressed by the enemy?

Psalm 42:5,9

Blue, low, sad, dejected, desolate, miserable, downhearted, unhappy. Those who suffer depression know that not one of these terms comes anywhere near describing your experiences of this chronic illness.

What Causes Depression?

Depression is a complex condition; a multi-faceted poisonous cocktail of biochemical, genetic, environmental and psychological factors that, despite much scientific research, still remains unclear.

BIOCHEMICAL FACTORS

There is a possible link between depression and an imbalance of the neurotransmitters serotonin, dopamine and norepinephrine. These chemical messengers are released and received by the brain's nerve cells (neurons), enabling different parts of the brain to communicate with each other. MRI scans show that in depressed people parts of the brain responsible for regulating mood, thought, sleep, appetite and behaviour function abnormally compared to the brains of those without depression. However, biochemical evidence is problematic, in that these observed imbalances may simply be the body's physical *response* to psychological depression and, therefore, not the *cause* of that depression.

GENETIC FACTORS

Bipolar and major depression seems to run in families. However, this appears to be an inherited *susceptibility* and not a certainty, as research shows that you may only be 1.5 to 3 times more likely to develop the condition than those who don't have a close relative with it. Research has yet to identify a clear link between a specific gene, or genes, and depression.

PSYCHOLOGICAL FACTORS

Those with low self-esteem and perfectionists are more prone to develop depression. These opposite ends of a spectrum – a negative outlook and unreasonably high expectations – can both result in frequent experiences of stress and becoming overwhelmed by them.

ENVIRONMENTAL FACTORS

Depression can be triggered by specific life events. For example, bereavement, job loss, relationship breakdown, serious illness, financial problems – situations that bring us rejection and/or loss. Having experienced traumatic, brutal or violent events, particularly in childhood, or living in situations that cause us ongoing and relentless stress, are further risk factors. In fact, any situation that leaves you feeling overwhelmed and challenges your ability to cope can lead you to experiencing depression.

Symptoms

The symptoms of depression are manifold, being both emotional and physical, and can persist for weeks, months, or even years. Several or all of the following will be experienced:

- Feeling hopeless and helpless – despair;
- Self-loathing – feeling worthless, unlovable and believing that you are a bad person;
- Guilt;
- Shame;

- Anxiety;
- Obsessive negative thoughts about yourself, the world, the future;
- Difficulty concentrating, remembering and making decisions;
- Loss of interest in daily activities;
- Feeling emotionally numb;
- Sleep disruption – insomnia or excessive sleeping;
- Abnormal appetite – anorexia or overeating;
- Apathy;
- Fatigue and tiredness;
- Headaches;
- Digestive problems;
- Muscular aches and joint pain; chest pain.

However, each person's experience of depression is uniquely their own and is extremely difficult to describe to anyone else. Depression is insidious, creeping into the mind over time until you find yourself consumed and overwhelmed by it. Many describe it as being locked in a dark prison cell. For me, I feel as if I am at the bottom of a deep pit, without knowing how I arrived at this point and from which I can see no escape. Life loses any joy or meaning, becoming a series of insurmountable obstacles that you don't want to face or deal with. You become totally self-focussed on your wretched feelings; the agonised, persistent inner scream that wants only to escape by going to a safe place – preferably oblivion. In this process you become isolated from others, emotionally numb to their needs and, strangely, detached from the real you, whom you may receive brief glimpses of, as of a distant memory. Divorced from what is going on around you, you become an actor in your own life. Of course, you believe that everything is your fault, that you are not good enough, successful enough, clever enough; in short, that you are a complete failure.

Looking at myself from the other side of a depressive episode, this is the best description I can try to relate to you. Your experience will be very different from mine. The following description by Kay Redfield Jamison, a clinical psychologist and Professor of Psychiatry at Johns Hopkins University, is the most complete I have found:

> *In its severe forms, depression paralyzes all of the otherwise vital forces that make us human, leaving instead a bleak, despairing,*

desperate and deadened state ... Life is bloodless, pulseless, and yet present enough to allow a suffocating horror and pain.[2]

There is a wide range of psychological and medical treatments for depression; the most common being Cognitive Behavioural Therapy (CBT), counselling, antidepressant drugs and electroconvulsive therapy (ECT).

There are now twenty-six antidepressant drugs in use worldwide and as many as 1 in 10 people are prescribed them in some countries. However, many people find that drug therapies do not work and have unacceptable side-effects: nausea, weight gain, fatigue, insomnia, headaches, blurred vision, anxiety, digestive problems, feeling 'spaced out' and divorced from the world. In a survey of 1,829 people using antidepressants, over half reported thoughts of suicide and emotional numbness.[3] Only one third of patients will experience remission of depressive symptoms after treatment, and successive treatments will only have a beneficial outcome for 20-25%. In fact, those using drug therapy are more likely to suffer a relapse of major depression than those using no medication.[4] Furthermore, scientific research has revealed that placebos work nearly as well as antidepressants.[5]

Similarly, the efficacy of CBT has been widely called into question in recent years. The outcome of seventy studies between 1977 and 2014, involving over 2,400 people, found that CBT's ability to reduce depressive symptoms is shrinking. This suggests that CBT had a placebo effect when it was widely believed to be the wonder cure.[6] Indeed, leading psychologist Oliver James has claimed that CBT is "a scam and a waste of money", finding that it has no lasting benefit: two years after treatment those who received it are no better than those

---

[2] Jamison, Kay Redfield, "An Unquiet Mind: A Memoir of Moods and Madness", (New York: Vintage Books, 1995)

[3] Read Professor John, et al, "Adverse emotional and interpersonal effects reported by 1,829 New Zealanders while taking antidepressants", Psychiatry Research, 2014; DOI: 10.1016/j psychres. 2014.01.042

[4] Friedman, Richard A., MD, "A New Focus on Depression", The New York Times, December 23, 2013

[5] Fournier, J.C., et al, University of Pennsylvania, 2010. Research conducted across 6 clinical trials.

[6] Johnsen, T., and Friborg, O., "The Effects of Cognitive Behavioural Therapy as an Anti-Depressive Treatment is Falling: A Meta-Analysis", Psychological Bulletin, Vol. 141(4), July 2015, 747-768

who didn't.[7] Many clinical trials have demonstrated that CBT produces no better outcomes than counselling.[8]

ECT, or Electric Shock Treatment, has been practised since 1938 and is used in treating depression when all else has failed. It is thought to have an impact on the function and effect of neurotransmitters within the brain. Reported side-effects include headaches and memory loss. Again, as with other treatments, relapse rates remain high: 37.7% within six months, 51.1% after twelve months.[9]

We can therefore conclude that all of these treatments 'work' for some people some of the time.

Why is their success so limited?

– Because they only treat the *symptoms* of depression. They do not address the underlying problems that will still be there to trigger further episodes.

Without realising it, we engage in habitual, ingrained ways of thinking and behaving that are destructive because they keep us apart from God: blame, worry and anxiety, despair, ingratitude.

The mind governed by the flesh is hostile to God.

Romans 8:7

It is the will of man that makes life hell. We are God's children (Romans 8:16). Just as a child suffers when deprived of a close and loving relationship with its parents, so God-deprivation makes us sick.

As you work through the following chapters, reading and meditating upon the Bible verses that illuminate the pathway out of depression, allow yourself to be washed with the Word; to be cleansed, healed and made new.

---

[7] Hope, Jenny, "'CBT is a scam and a waste of money': Popular talking therapy is not a long-term solution, says leading psychologist," The Daily Mail, 10th November, 2014

[8] For example, Lynch et al, 2010; Jones et al, 2012; Jauhar et al, 2014.

[9] Jelovac, A., et al, "Relapse Following Successful Electroconvulsive Therapy for Major Depression: A Meta-Analysis", Neuropsychopharmacology (2013), 38, 2467-2474. The Medical College of Georgia at Georgia Regents University also found a six-month relapse in a study of 500 people.

...to put off your old self, which is being corrupted by its deceitful desires; to be made new in the attitude of your minds.

Ephesians 4:22-23

Above all, although I know that at this moment you may find this very hard to believe or understand, remember that God loves you! You are His child, He knows you individually and He does care:

The LORD sets prisoners free ... the LORD lifts up those who are bowed down.

Psalm 146:7-8

Blame

Whose fault is it? Who is responsible for this? Where does the blame lie? We ask these questions so often on a daily basis that we barely give them a second thought. Have you noticed how so much of our news media coverage centres on apportioning blame, especially in the wake of tragic, catastrophic or violent events? When something goes wrong, it would seem that we have a deep need to explain what caused it. Invariably this means holding someone or a group of people responsible; finding their actions to be socially or morally irresponsible. We live in a blame culture where sitting in judgment has become habitual. We also do this within our personal lives as we seek to make sense of what happens to us, particularly something which has caused us loss, pain or fear. If we can't find others responsible, we turn that blame upon ourselves. As we will discover, blame is a major feature of depression: self-blame; being a victim of blame; blaming others.

Jesus is Calling You

Chapter Two

Self-Blame

Self-blame is the key factor in depression. It has two aspects: shame and guilt.

Shame

But I am a worm and not a man, scorned by everyone, despised by the people.

Psalm 22:6

Shame is a sense of *being* wrong; feeling inferior, untouchable, dirty, unlovable. You believe that there is something so fundamentally bad about you, that you don't deserve to be happy. But where do such feelings of self-loathing come from? We are not born with them. Remember, we are God's children, created in perfection.

See what great love the Father has lavished on us, that we should be called children of God! And that is what we are!

1 John 3:1

For he chose us in him before the creation of the world to be holy and blameless in his sight.

Ephesians 1:4

Low self-esteem is a learned behaviour. It often has its roots in childhood. During our developmental years the judgments made of us by others become the way in which we regard ourselves into adulthood. So if you were seen as worthless and unimportant, you will internalise this idea of yourself, believing that no one loves you because you are not worth loving. If you were constantly criticised for apparent failings, you will lack confidence in your abilities and become overly self-critical. Very often during childhood we do not understand events, particularly traumatic ones, that happen around and to us. Unless adults take the time and care to explain, a child, being by nature egocentric, will take on responsibility for the bad thing that happened. They will blame themselves, thinking that they in some way caused it. This erroneous belief will then be carried through life as a source of constant anguish.

Being habitually self-critical is one of the key ways depression becomes reinforced and entrenched. This is particularly linked to perfectionism. Setting impossibly high standards for ourselves can only lead to repeated experiences of failure. This, in turn, heightens feelings of worthlessness, leading to self-hatred and seeing oneself as a failure. Another feature of perfectionism is a tendency to take on too much personal responsibility. If we believe that events are within our control, and perfectionism demands this, then it follows that everything becomes our fault.

Self-Punishment

Carl Jung, the founder of analytical psychology, believed that shame is a soul-eating emotion. Its destructive effect can be seen in the self-punishment that is a characteristic of depression. This can range from negative self-talk to self-attack in the form of addiction, eating disorders, seeking and remaining in abusive relationships, self-harming and suicidal thoughts. When we listen to that critical inner voice telling us that we are a worthless, stupid failure, we give it power over us. Truly believing we suffer because we deserve to be punished, we become ensnared in a cycle of behaviour based on low self-esteem that actually perpetuates and deepens it.

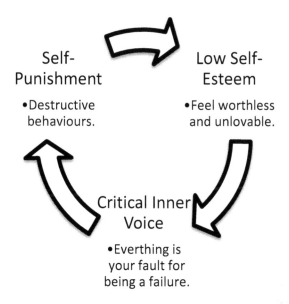

Figure 1: The cycle of low self-esteem

God's Healing Word

A man with leprosy came to him and begged him on his knees, "If you are willing, you can make me clean." Jesus ... reached out his hand and touched the man. "I am willing," he said. "Be clean!"

Mark 1:40-41

This man's anguished plea to be made clean resonates deeply with anyone who feels shame. He has been made to feel dirty, contaminated and untouchable by the society in which he lives and also by himself. Leprosy was, and sadly in many cultures still is, seen as a punishment from God for sinful behaviour. He is therefore regarded as worthy of disgrace and disapproval, leading to his being discriminated against and excluded. In turn, he has internalised his experience and perception of this stigmatisation, resulting in his evident shame. Surrounded by people who tell him and show him that he is 'bad', he believes this to be true. As we saw earlier, low self-esteem, a lack of self-love, is rooted in our listening to and accepting others' judgments upon us.

However, this man recognises what we all need to realise: only God can heal us ("you can make me clean"). Furthermore, it is not a case of *if*; God *is* willing! All we have to do is seek God's help in prayer.

Did you notice how the man with leprosy is in a physical attitude of prayer and supplication? Jesus assures us:

> *Ask and it will be given to you; seek and you will find; knock and the door will be opened to you.*
>
> Matthew 7:7

Christ meets us where we are, here and now.

In touching the untouchable man, Jesus demonstrates how meaningless our man-made concept of shame is. Filled with compassion for this abused and broken man, Jesus' touch of love reassures us that no one is beyond God's love; nothing can separate us from it (Romans 8:38-39). There is no shame before God. You are His much-loved, holy and blameless, perfect child. Be clean! Upon Christ's touch, being wrong becomes being pure, whole and loved.

Still feeling like a worthless failure? To whom are you listening?

The misery caused by low self-esteem arises from trying to live up to the expectations of others. That self-critical inner voice comes from listening to the world's values regarding 'success', based on the acquisition of wealth and possessions and arbitrary standards of intelligence and beauty. We self-judge and self-disapprove based on these man-made ideals. If we don't match up to them, we feel like we've failed. But striving after success and trying to please other people is a fool's errand. Material things do not last and, as we've seen in recent years, wealth can be wiped out in an instant. You can't listen to the world and listen to God at the same time! God's ways and ours are not the same.

> *No one can serve two masters. Either you will hate the one and love the other, or you will be devoted to the one and despise the other.*
>
> Matthew 6:24a

> *Do not put your trust in ... human beings, who cannot save.*
>
> Psalm 146:3

Our concepts of shame and success do not stand up to scrutiny in the light of God's will. Jesus shows us a different way: be content with what you have, because God provides for all your needs and knows what you need. This point is beautifully illustrated at the end of Luke chapter 10 when Jesus and his disciples visit Martha and Mary. While

Mary sits at Jesus' feet listening to what he has to say, her sister is totally distracted by everyday minutiae – the ways of the world.

> *"Martha, Martha," [Jesus calls to her,] "you are worried and upset about many things, but few things are needed – or indeed only one."*
>
> Luke 10:41-42

Mary has chosen the better path by listening to God; something that can never be taken away from her.

How do we listen to God? Through reading His Word and prayer. Don't forget, Christ meets us where we are. God's presence is with us at all times and in all places. You can meet with Him wherever you are.

Don't Be so Hard on Yourself: Overcoming Shame

BECOME AWARE

Acknowledging your low self-esteem and understanding how it developed is the beginning of your healing.

LOVE YOURSELF

When we read the parables[10] of Jesus' healings, we see that his immediate response to those in need is always that of compassion. God is our supportive and encouraging parent. His love for us is unconditional. Rarely do we show ourselves such kindness and understanding.

SELF-COMPASSION

Self-love is not a sin! Caring for yourself does not mean that you are being self-centred, totally focused upon yourself to the exclusion of all else.

- *Learn* to accept and love yourself as you are. After all, you are God's perfect child.

---

[10] The term 'parables' is used in relation to Jesus' healings deliberately. Jesus used parables in his teaching as an aid to open people's eyes to reality, if they chose to do so. I believe that the healings demonstratively fulfilled this function.

- *Recognise* that punishing yourself does not change you; it simply perpetuates and deepens low self-esteem.
- *Understand* that shame is man-made. You are not responsible for living up to other people's expectations. You may hear their critical views of you, but you do not have to listen to them. Listening means accepting their negativity.[11]

Guilt

My guilt has overwhelmed me like a burden too heavy to bear.

Psalm 38:4

Guilt is a feeling of responsibility for doing something wrong that can be real or imagined. We believe that our actions have caused or might cause harm. This aspect of self-blame is all about, "I should have done _____ differently."

Guilt is normal. It is a warning signal that lets us know when we have broken social and moral rules, when we have offended and hurt others. We deal with it by admitting our wrongdoing, apologising, rectifying the situation if possible and seeking forgiveness. We learn from this by improving our behaviour and moving on. So, this type of *rational* guilt is good for us. However, the low self-esteem of depression carries with it vast quantities of *irrational* guilt: feeling guilty about things that are not our fault.

An example of this type of guilt is found in the grieving process. Part of grief is searching for an explanation as to why the person died. In this emotionally overwhelming situation we may feel that it was because we failed in our duties towards the deceased. For example, we did something wrong that contributed to their death. We didn't notice their symptoms or waited too long to seek treatment. We didn't comfort them enough when they were ill. We weren't there when they died. We feel guilty for being relieved that their suffering is over. We may even feel guilt because we survived them. By feeling guilty we take on responsibility for the death: "Because I did/didn't do _____,

---

[11] For more on self-compassion visit *theselfcompassionproject.com.*

this happened." Through taking this responsibility we regain a sense of control in the face of an unpredictable world.[12]

This highlights two key aspects of irrational guilt: responsibility and control. Taking on excessive responsibility for everything that happens, especially bad things, gives us a sense of control when we don't have it, particularly in situations in which we feel powerless. Therefore, we think in this way in order to comfort ourselves. However, being over-responsible leads to becoming over-conscientious and oversensitive. If the buck always stops with you, it follows that it is your duty to make everything right and perfect, and to keep everyone else happy in the process. Quite a tall order!

In fact, any comfort is very short-lived because you are using the guilt to control yourself. That critical inner voice of low self-esteem makes sure that you punish yourself with guilt. When you have a sense of obligation for pleasing others (making everything right), if they are unhappy it must be your fault, so you feel guilty. When you make a mistake or things don't go to plan or, horror of horrors, something goes wrong, you self-punish for never being good enough. This way of thinking results in putting yourself under unreasonable and, eventually, intolerable pressure. Any criticism, however slight, you take personally and it wounds you to the core; evidence, once more, of your failure to be perfect. You find yourself unable to make decisions for fear of getting it wrong or upsetting people. You believe that there is only one right way of doing things. You constantly ruminate on the past, torturing yourself with your perceived failures. This is a destructive pattern of behaviour that serves only to plunge you into despair and depression.

Being Blamed

Being blamed for something you didn't do or for something that was entirely beyond your control is a form of emotional abuse.

Being told, "It's your fault." = "You are guilty."

If this message is then constantly reinforced, you may come to believe that you *are* responsible. This is known as 'scapegoating' – being forced to take the blame for someone else's problems, thereby

---

[12] Two helpful websites if you are grieving: *www.whatsyourgrief.com; www.healingheart.net.*

becoming the target for their anger about their own failures. The origin of the scapegoat is found in Leviticus, chapter 16, when God instructed Moses and Aaron to sacrifice two goats. The blood of one was sprinkled on the Ark of the Covenant, but Aaron was to lay his hands on the head of the second and confess the sins of the people upon it. This 'scapegoat' was then released into the wilderness to carry the burden of Israel's sin.

Have you been made a scapegoat? Within the family, this often begins in childhood when you become the object of everyone's blame; constantly put down, picked on and even ostracised. Believing what you are repeatedly told about yourself, you accept the blame and grow into a self-hating, depressed adult. Workplace bullying operates in exactly the same way. This is a serious and growing problem across the UK, USA, Canada and Australia. A UK helpline received over 20,000 calls in one year, with some callers reporting that bullying had caused them to self-harm or consider suicide.[13]

If you are, or have been, in one of these situations, it is important to recognise that you have been given a responsibility for others' actions and reactions that is not yours to own. You have received and accepted *their* guilt. Of course, the true function of the scapegoat is to take away people's fears. Within the workplace, the perpetrator is invariably trying to deflect responsibility away from themselves for mistakes they have made. In the family, scapegoating can be an expression of a parent's own mental health issues, or a way of hiding deeper family problems.

God's Healing Word

Then I acknowledged my sin to you and did not cover up my iniquity. I said, "I will confess my transgressions to the LORD." And you forgave the guilt of my sin.

Psalm 32:5

Repent and live! Be assured, God will forgive you whatever you have done. His forgiveness is always there for those who seek it in repentance. Repentance means 'a change of mind' – us, deciding to

---

[13] See "Acas study reveals that workplace bullying is on the rise", Monday 16th November, 2015, *www.acas.org.uk*

change our ways; God, cleansing and renewing us in mind, heart and spirit.

The first step is *confession;* acknowledging to God and ourselves that we have done wrong. Then, we make a conscious decision to turn away from that wrongdoing and return to God.

> *Come near to God and he will come near to you.*
>
> James 4:8

Why does God forgive us, wiping out all our sins and healing us?

– Because "he will renew you in his love"[14], and that love is steadfast, everlasting and unconditional.

This forgiveness applies equally to rational and irrational guilt. After all, if God can forgive you, you can forgive yourself.

> *Trust in the LORD with all your heart and lean not on your own understanding; in all your ways submit to him, and he will make your paths straight.*
>
> Proverbs 3:5-6

At those times in life when you are feeling helpless and overwhelmed you need to take a step back and stop. You are feeling this way because you feel out of control, and that's scary. But get used to it. You are powerless! It is not your responsibility to control and shape events. God asks us to trust Him. We can do this with absolute confidence because...

> *...we know that in all things God works for the good of those who love him.*
>
> Romans 8:28

And, even though life may seem very bleak, we can also be certain that God is working His purpose out because He has sworn:

> *Surely, as I have planned, so it will be, and as I have purposed, so it will happen.*
>
> Isaiah 14:24

So, when you're going through bad times and you're tempted to say, "Why is this happening to me? It must be my fault. I deserve to be punished," hold on to these facts: God's goodness, His omnipotence and His love. He has a plan for each of us. It is only by having our faith

---

[14] Zephaniah 3:17 (RSV)

tested that it can become stronger. The Apostle Paul had his faith tested many times. He pleaded with God for it to end, but the Lord told him:

> *My grace is sufficient for you, for my power is made perfect in weakness.*
>
> 2 Corinthians 12:9-10

Instead of trying to be self-dependent, which only leads to punishing ourselves with irrational guilt over our failure to be in control of everything, we can rely totally on God's strength. By taking our troubles (weakness) to God and depending on Him as our refuge and fortress, faith grows. In giving control back to God we are freed from the burden of all-encompassing responsibility. Faith and freedom bring us peace of mind.

> *The tongue ... corrupts the whole body, sets the whole course of one's life on fire, and is itself set on fire by hell. ... It is a restless evil, full of deadly poison.*
>
> James 3:6,8

By listening to the world, we agree to be a victim. Guilt is the voice of the world. We sit in judgment on each other, finding fault, accusing and apportioning blame. It would appear that we cannot tame our tongues! As we have learned, the critical inner voice of low self-esteem, the basis of depression, tends to develop during childhood when we accept the judgments made of us by our significant others (parents, siblings, extended family and teachers). Because of what people say to us, we take on responsibilities for their feelings and their expectations.

But when we listen to God, we experience a different attitude of mind. We need to listen carefully for that still, small voice, the gentle whisper that can be difficult to hear above the clamour of our noise. Jesus tells us:

> *My sheep listen to my voice; ... and they follow me.*
>
> John 10:27

It is the voice of love engendering compassion and forgiveness.

In our world these qualities are sidelined, if not sneered at, as a sign of weakness. But when we are eaten up by guilt, we aren't accepting God's love for us; a love that replaces punishment with forgiveness; a love that exhorts us not only to serve each other, but to care for ourselves too (see Matthew 22:37-9). Because if you can't love yourself, how can you give love to others?

Lifting the Burden: Overcoming Guilt

- Acknowledge and analyse your guilt. Look for its origin, then you can start to deal with it appropriately.
- You aren't perfect! No one can get everything right all the time because we live in a world of uncertainty. We learn by making mistakes. So, forgive yourself!
- Get rid of constant self-judgment by not ruminating on past mistakes or perceived failures – all the 'should haves'. You have to accept that you cannot change the past. But you can change how you feel and behave now.
- Work out what is and is not your responsibility; what you do and don't have control over.
  You *don't* have the power to control the feelings and actions of others. Therefore, you *don't* have the responsibility of guilt.
  You *can* take responsibility for your actions and attitude. Don't agree to be a victim!

CHAPTER THREE

Blaming Others and Past Events

I loathe my very life; therefore I will give free rein to my complaint and speak out in the bitterness of my soul.

Job 10:1

Blame is a form of punishment. When we are feeling hurt, sad or angry it is as a result of some kind of injury, loss or insult we have suffered. Someone must be responsible for making us feel this way. So it's only right that they should be punished in return for the wrong done to us. After all, they are to blame. As a society we believe in the efficacy of punishing the perpetrator in order to gain justice for the victim. But isn't there an element of lashing out and seeking revenge in this process of retribution? By pointing the finger of blame at someone when they hurt us, we identify them as being 'bad'; they have transgressed our values and not met our expectations of them. In this way, we gain control over them. They are wrong, we are right; they are malicious, we are the innocent victim of their harm.

However, in blaming others and past events for the way we feel now – our depression – we operate from two mistaken beliefs. Firstly, that *one* person, group, decision or event caused something to happen to us. Usually, there are many factors that played a part. Secondly, that results only follow from a *deliberate intent.* By holding others responsible for our feelings, we lock them in a prison of blame, from which there is no escape, and ourselves too by constantly dwelling on our injured state.

In fact, we render ourselves victims. We have come to feel helpless in the face of misfortune or ill-treatment. This is a common feature of depression. When you see yourself as a victim, you are angry. You think that you are being punished. As we have seen, those with low self-esteem believe that they deserve such punishment. Just like low self-esteem, the *victim mentality* is a learned behaviour, whereby we regard ourselves as a victim of the negative actions of others. We learn to be helpless. Again, this often originates in childhood, when we were relatively powerless. In adulthood it serves us as a defence mechanism; a way of deflecting responsibility away from ourselves onto more 'powerful' people and events that we are at the mercy of. It also fulfils the childish function of an attention-seeking strategy, as our victim status elicits pity and sympathy from others that we crave. Receiving sympathy is pleasurable; it makes us feel loved and valued.

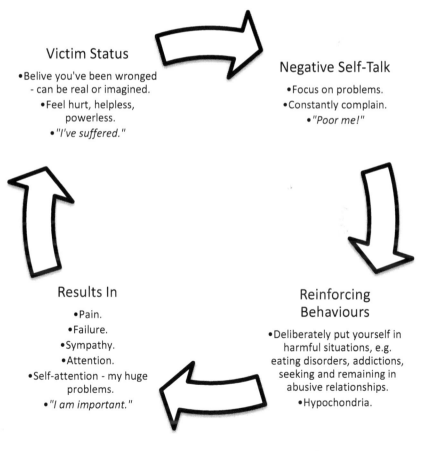

Victim Status

- Belive you've been wronged - can be real or imagined.
- Feel hurt, helpless, powerless.
- *"I've suffered."*

Negative Self-Talk

- Focus on problems.
- Constantly complain.
- *"Poor me!"*

Results In

- Pain.
- Failure.
- Sympathy.
- Attention.
- Self-attention - my huge problems.
- *"I am important."*

Reinforcing Behaviours

- Deliberately put yourself in harmful situations, e.g. eating disorders, addictions, seeking and remaining in abusive relationships.
- Hypochondria.

Figure 2: The cycle of victimhood

27

Victim mentality is reinforced in a number of ways:

- *By negative self-talk.* This is comprised of fear, sadness, suspicion of other people, suppressed anger and self-pity.
- *By what others tell you.* When people treat you badly, it is indicative of their own problems. You don't have to accept what they say as being true. But when you have low self-esteem you will, because it reinforces your own view of yourself and makes you the victim. Or, if they say, "Poor you, how dreadful," etc, this gives you the attention you seek whilst at the same time confirming your victim status.
- *By getting stuck in the past.* You constantly dwell on past hurts thereby reliving the negative feelings associated with them. Indeed, your victim mentality is a self-perpetuating cycle.

God's Healing Word

If someone slaps you on one cheek, turn to them the other also.

Luke 6:29

Can someone else or an event cause our feelings? Most of us would answer yes. Indeed, it would appear that I have been suggesting that childhood experiences and upbringing are responsible for adult depression. Certainly, the roots of our depression may be found there, but we are responsible for our *own* feelings. You can't blame your parents, teachers, boss or spouse! We cause our emotions because of the way we think – our beliefs and expectations. How often do we say, "It's his/her fault I feel…" when blaming others for our negative feelings? Don't we just love to point the finger of blame in order to avoid facing the fact that we *allow* our feelings? When we say that how we feel is someone's fault, what we really mean is, "You are wrong," so that, by comparison, "I am right." Our pride obscures the reality that we choose how we respond to events. We *can* control what we believe. Viktor Frankl, an Austrian psychologist and neurologist, identified that there is a gap between what someone says or does and our response to that. It is in this gap that we have a choice.[15]

---

[15] See Frankl, Viktor E., "Man's Search for Meaning", (1946; Beacon Press, Boston, 2006)

Popular opinion tells us that we must be assertive and not allow others to dominate us. But Jesus shows us a different way: when we *own* our feelings, we can 'turn the other cheek'. We can subsume that sense of self that relies on pride for its validation. Because if we accept responsibility for our own negative emotions, it doesn't matter what other people say or do to us. There is no wounded pride. No need to take revenge. It gets rid of blame.

> *"Lord, how many times shall I forgive my brother or sister who sins against me? Up to seven times?"*
> *Jesus answered, "I tell you, not seven times, but seventy-seven times."*
>
> Matthew 18:21-2

On Wednesday, 17th June, 2015, a young man, motivated and misguided by hatred, shot dead nine worshippers at Emanuel African Methodist Episcopal Church in Charleston, South Carolina. Prior to the attack, he had been welcomed by the same people into a Bible study class.

Following his arrest, when he appeared in court, relatives of the deceased were allowed to address him. Something remarkable happened. Instead of a tirade of pain, grief and their own hatred of him, they forgave him. More than this, they told him that they were praying for his salvation. At the church service on the following Sunday, thousands of people gathered, held hands and prayed. There were no race riots, no demonstrations, no mass unrest. What a powerful example of love and forgiveness in action.[16]

Forgiveness is a two-way street:

> *For if you forgive other people when they sin against you, your heavenly Father will also forgive you.*
>
> Matthew 6:14

Apart from the certainty that God will forgive us, why should we forgive?

– Because it is the antidote to blame.

---

[16] For a moving account of this incident see, 'Here's My View: The aftermath of a tragedy: Christian love triumphs over satanic evil', by Tommy Campbell, Editor, The Rogersville Review, 24 June, 2015

Jesus knew that bearing grudges ties us to the past, preventing us from moving forwards in the freedom of a love that enables real living. Blame eats us up with anger and resentment, even a desire for revenge. Mired in such negativity, no wonder we become depressed!

The aftermath of the Charleston shooting exemplifies how to forgive: loving your enemy, doing good to people who hate you, blessing and praying for those who behave badly towards you (see Luke 6:27-8). And, no, this isn't easy! It goes against all our desires; desires that emanate from pride of self. It is important to understand that this is not the same as self-esteem. The latter is about loving yourself as God's child; the former comes from putting the demands of your selfish will above all else. But when you practise owning your feelings, forgiveness becomes a whole lot easier; bringing real healing, not just to others, but to you as well. If you want to be happy, forgive and forgive and forgive!

I Am Not a Victim: Overcoming Blame

- You have control of your feelings; no one and nothing else does.
- When you find yourself blaming, take a moment. Analyse your feelings and take control; admit ownership.
- Say how you feel connected to what you have *observed* only, instead of your interpretation of what happened. For example, "I am upset that you did _____," rather than, "I feel you _____ me."
- You are not a victim! As adults we can choose how we respond to people and events. We don't have to continue to be the little child seething with unexpressed anger and resentment.
- You aren't responsible for other people's feelings. They are. Therefore, you don't have to 'fix' their anger and unhappiness.
- When we accept that each person owns their own negative emotions, it gets rid of blame.
- Let go of the past. Other people and events are not responsible for how we feel now. The past is dead and gone. Don't try to keep it alive. Maybe you were hurt, but it is over now.
- Above all, forgive. If you can't do this actively, at the very least forget and move on. Don't allow your selfish pride to overwhelm the freedom that a loving attitude can bring.

CHAPTER FOUR

Whose Way?

We all, like sheep, have gone astray, each of us has turned to our own way.

Isaiah 53:6

The origin of the word 'blame' is revealing. It comes from 'blaspheme', to speak irreverently about God; which comes from the Greek 'blasphemos', which means evil-speaking. So, that is what we are *really* doing when we blame others and ourselves.

How do we know this to be true?

– Because blame is destructive; it is predicated upon punishment. Think of the effects of shame and guilt: self-loathing, self-criticism and the self-harming behaviours these lead to; the abusive effects of being made a scapegoat. Or, seeking revenge when we've been hurt. Or, the negativity of a victim mentality that results in us nurturing resentment and anger.

It is by going our own way that such destruction ensues. When we insist that we are in control, not God, trouble is sure to follow. Remember:

In this world you will have trouble.

John 16:33

Instead of facing up to our essential powerlessness, and placing our trust in God, we try to cope with our uncertain world by making ourselves, or someone else, responsible for everything. Of course we become depressed when the controlling aspects of perfectionism and irrational guilt only result in a vicious cycle of repeated failure and punishment. When we are motivated by pride and a self-centred will, we don't forgive. Unforgiveness leads to hatred and self-pity. End result: we become depressed.

Listening to man instead of God, placing our man-made concepts above God's commandments, is always a recipe for disaster. Guilt and shame are 'stones' we carry around with us that drag us down into depression. Humanity has devised them as a means of control. We lock ourselves in a prison of blame with unforgiveness as the key that keeps us there.

Love Frees; Evil Imprisons

Blame keeps us apart from God because it does not emanate from love and nothing good comes from it. Paul tells us:

> *Hate what is evil; cling to what is good. Be devoted to one another in love. Honour one another above yourselves.*
> Romans 12:9-10

God's way is love. Love comes from God because God is love. The destructiveness of blame is counteracted by forgiveness. Forgive others. Forgive yourself. Forgive the past and let it go. Forgiveness is God speaking; an expression of divine love. It brings healing. When we forgive, others are released from the judgment of blame and we are freed from the negative aspects of our depression: resentment, anger, hatred, pain and anguish. Living in love, expressing and reflecting it, brings us back into a right relationship with God.

You have the choice. Whose way are you going to follow? Your own, someone else's or God's?

> *Do not be overcome by evil, but overcome evil with good.*
> Romans 12:21

Worry and Anxiety

Recent years have witnessed an epidemic of worry and anxiety. 30% of mental health problems seen by G.P.s in the UK are anxiety-related. 1 in 20 adults are affected by an anxiety disorder. Research conducted by the NHS Information Centre showed that outpatient appointments for anxiety disorders totalled 3,754 in 2006-7, but by 2010-11 there had been a huge increase to 17,470[17] and in 2015 appointments topped a million for the first time.[18] Financial uncertainty has been cited as the main cause of this meteoric rise. However, this is not the whole picture.

Today, we live in a climate of worry and fear. As an interesting exercise, count how many times you hear and see the words worry/worries and fear/fears over the course of a week's news coverage. As examples: "Prospect of Brexit worries Germany"; "Worrying decline in 40-year-olds saving for their retirement"; "Experts fear ISIS terrorist knifemen will target Western Church for their next attack".[19] Notice how everything is worrying and fears are always growing, never decreasing! We are constantly being encouraged to worry and be afraid. In fact, worrying has become endemic and habitual. Our children and teenagers are under unprecedented pressure to perform academically and to worry if they aren't making the grade. Recent financial crises have led many into permanent money worries. We are bombarded with a regular diet of health scares, global warming fears, Brexit fallout and impending doom.

As we will learn in the following chapter, worry and anxiety are inextricably linked to depression.

---

[17] Qureshi, Huma, "Clinical anxiety is becoming a worry", The Guardian, 19 May, 2013

[18] *digital.nhs.uk,* "Psychological Therapies: Annual Report on the use of Improving Access to Psychological Therapies services, England, 2014/15", 24 November, 2015

[19] BBC News, June 5, 2016; The Daily Express, September 7, 2016; The Mirror, August 30, 2016

Jesus is Calling You

CHAPTER FIVE

Worry and Anxiety

The churning inside me never stops; days of suffering confront me.

Job 30:27

Worry

When we worry, we allow our minds to dwell on difficulties and troubles, problems and fears. Because we tend to worry about specific problems that can't currently be solved, this negative thought can quickly become repetitive and obsessive.

So, why do we do it? The things we worry about fall into three broad categories:

- Loss – of wealth, power, status, love, freedom, happiness and health.
- Making decisions – the importance of 'getting it right'.
- Being judged and criticised – what other people think of us.

We learn to worry from a very young age. Seeing our parents worrying in particular, as well as the behaviour of other family members and friends, gives us the example of worrying being the right thing to do when you have a problem. Overprotective parenting produces insecure children, who grow into worrying, anxious adults. The child who is under constant scrutiny from the hovering parent, determined to protect them from any sort of harm and making mistakes, becomes stressed and anxious. The whole message they are receiving from their parents is, "You aren't capable of doing things for yourself; we don't trust you to get it right." However well-intentioned their parents' behaviour may be, the child is not allowed to be independent, handling situations for themselves, and therefore does not develop the self-confidence that comes from this. This scenario also results in the perfectionist adult who needs to be in control of absolutely everything at all times, and spends their life worrying about how to achieve this.

Many people believe that worrying is actually good for them. They think that it helps them to come up with solutions to their problems, or that they can somehow protect themselves by preparing for the worst. Furthermore, social pressure encourages us to worry. Being 'responsible' parents, students, workers requires that we should be worrying about our children; achieving ever higher grades; meeting performance targets.

If worrying is so good, why are its effects so bad? There is no doubt that worrying can have serious consequences for our physical health: raised blood pressure and heart rate, panic attacks, digestive problems, IBS, nausea, disturbed sleep, insomnia and fatigue, dizziness and headaches. Moreover, worrying leads to anxiety. When we don't know how to solve the problems we are faced with, we feel that we have lost control. Our thoughts become extremely negative, focused on what we believe can only be impending doom, and we enter a state of persistent anxiety.

Anxiety

Anxiety is experienced as uncontrolled, unrestrained fear that becomes constant and overwhelming. Unlike worry, which is specific, anxiety is generalised. We believe and expect that something bad is going to happen. Why do we think this way?

At the heart of anxiety is uncertainty about the future. In an attempt to feel safe, we want to control what is going to happen. So, we look out for possible danger, anticipating and trying to prevent what we perceive as a threat. It is important to recognise that when we are anxious we are being controlled by fear:

- Of harm to ourselves and loved ones;
- Of losing control and the ability to achieve desired goals;

- Of losing power and prestige;
- Of being criticised, shamed, disliked or rejected.

Motivated by fear, our need to be in control of the future simply produces even more fear! In order to be prepared for any eventuality, we use our imaginations to create scenarios of threats to our security and self-worth, and possible outcomes. We imagine all kinds of threats which, in turn, generate feelings associated with them: apprehension, dread, worry and panic. A feature of anxiety is rumination. This is continuous, repetitive and compulsive thinking about the possible causes and consequences of an upsetting situation, which could be real or imagined. If we are constantly thinking about and replaying past emotional traumas, as well as imagined future ones, we are living all the feelings we have about these events. So, we are perpetually in a state of adrenaline-fuelled fight or flight. The physical effects of this range from unpleasant to dangerous; tension, mood swings, fatigue, headaches, high blood pressure, irregular heartbeat and possible heart attack. Moreover, your whole outlook on life becomes distorted by fear. When we are afraid we go into panic mode. We do not see things as they really are and we do not think rationally.

Fears and anxieties are learned behaviours; a conditioned response to avoid either the physical or mental pain of punishment. For example, we very quickly learn as children not to touch something hot because it hurts and injures us. Having been burned once, we avoid doing it again. It is just the same with emotional pain. We don't want to be hurt (punished), so we avoid anything that will cause this. Our lives then become based on avoidance behaviours. We measure our self-worth against this ability to avoid harm, loss of control and power, and being criticised. We fear failing to manage future events and their outcomes in this respect. Some seek relief from the unending pressure this generates in alcohol and other drugs, self-harming, compulsive behaviour and OCD (Obsessive Compulsive Disorder).[20]

Anxiety precedes depression. Surveys have long shown that 60-70% of people diagnosed with depression also experience anxiety symptoms or disorders. The basis of this link is our overestimation of

---

[20] For more on fear, anxiety and OCD, see P. A. Kennan, "OCD: Be Still and Know", (Leatherhead: Onwards and Upwards Publishers, 2015), ISBN 978-1-910197-66-0

risk and danger and underestimation of our ability to cope. Ultimately, all our efforts to be in control are bound to fail because they are unrealistic. How can you control something that hasn't happened yet and probably won't? What does happen is that we become imprisoned by fear. Rumination, negative, intrusive and obsessive thoughts make everything seem hopeless and you feel out of control. So, you withdraw from life; the ultimate act of avoidance.

CHAPTER SIX

Trust Him! – Overcoming Worry and Anxiety

God's Healing Word

...do not worry about your life, what you will eat; or about your body, what you will wear. For life is more than food, and the body more than clothes.

Luke 12:22-3

So much of what we worry about concerns loss of one sort or another: material possessions, or the ability to acquire them; status, esteem and self-worth; power and control; security; physical needs not being met.

Why do we think that God, who loves us, will take things away from us? Do we believe that we deserve to be punished in this way? This is wrong thinking. God provides for His children; not just enough, but in *abundance*. We lack nothing, having all the essentials of life such as oxygen, sunlight, water, plants, seeds and animals to provide us with food. But God's provision exceeds our basic needs. Water doesn't simply satisfy our thirst and irrigate crops; it creates a beautiful and dramatic landscape for our pleasure and wonder. Fertile soil enables the growth of a cornucopia of foodstuffs way beyond our nutritional requirements. There are rich, sweet, sour and salty flavours to excite the taste buds. The scents and colours of a vast array of flora and the diversity of fauna with which we share our planet all combine to delight our senses and provide never-ending interest.

Therefore, we can rest assured that God will meet all our needs. This is of key importance: what we *need,* rather than what we *want.* Most of what we desire is superficial, based largely on material possessions. These are the things the world tells us we should want; symbols that confirm wealth and confer status. They do not matter! You can live perfectly well without the latest iPhone, computer, car, etc. Happiness comes from being content with what you have. And what you have is what you need because...

> *...your Father knows what you need before you ask him.*
>
> Matthew 6:8

And what you have is thanks to God, not to your own power, intelligence or perceived 'luck', because it is God who gives us the ability to be productive and creative.

> *Can any one of you by worrying add a single hour to your life?*
>
> Matthew 6:27

Worry is of absolutely no use. It does not change what has happened, nor will it influence what might take place in the future. We are far better concentrating on the day at hand. Worrying about the future makes it more difficult to deal with today because your mind is distracted by things which may never happen anyway.

Figure 3: Beware of succumbing to the dictatorship of fear!

This is a chain reaction. The obvious advice would be to nip worry in the bud by avoiding doing it, so that the chain is broken. Sounds simple and easy, doesn't it? Not so straightforward in reality, though. This is because avoidance in the form of thought suppression does not work. Trying to forget about something that is worrying us just makes the anxious thought come back all the more. This is due to what psychologists term "thought rebound". In fact, avoidance and thought suppression reinforce fear.[21] Just trying to blank out our worry is like sticking a plaster over a wound. The 'wound', the root of our fear, is still there festering. Fear needs to be tackled head on.

As we learned in the previous chapter, the basis of anxiety is fear. Specifically, fear of the future; we can only foresee disaster befalling us.

Why is this?

– Because fear does not emanate from love. In fact, it takes us away from God. Nothing good comes from fear. All our negative, destructive emotions are generated by it; anger, frustration, hatred, aggression, violence and rage. When we are feeling hopeless, we even question and doubt God's love for us.

> *When I am afraid, I put my trust in you.*
>
> Psalm 56:3

The only way we can overcome worry and anxiety is by actively trusting God. What does this mean?

1. ACCEPTING HIS LOVE FOR US

God's love is there always; His help is readily available. We need to open ourselves up to this love and be prepared to receive it. This is a love that will not let us go. It holds us firm and secure. When you can really acknowledge this, it will become your anchor in life.

2. KNOWING THAT HIS PLANS ARE FOR GOOD

> *For I know the plans I have for you, says the LORD, plans for welfare and not for evil, to give you a future and a hope.*
>
> Jeremiah 29:11 (RSV)

We can be sure of this because God is omnipotent:

> *I am the LORD, and there is no other, apart from me there is no God.*
>
> Isaiah 45:5

Moreover, nothing and no one can separate us from, or prevent, the love of God that is working His purpose out:

---

[21] For more on thought suppression see, Dean, Jeremy, "Why Thought Suppression is Counter-Productive", PsyBlog, May 2009

> *...neither death, nor life, neither angels nor demons, neither the present nor the future, nor any powers...*
>
> Romans 8:38

Nothing can ever stop this.

3. RELYING ON GOD'S STRENGTH

To paraphrase Martin Luther, "Let God do the worrying." We don't have to solve every problem, get everything right and perfect for everyone all of the time, endlessly worrying about the decisions we make.

And why not?

– Because we are not alone.

> *Cast all your anxiety on him because he cares for you.*
>
> 1 Peter 5:7

Listen for His voice. Prayer is answered. He will encourage, strengthen and help you. It is through prayer that we establish and maintain a relationship and partnership with God.

Relying totally on ourselves inevitably keeps us apart from God, because we are following our own will rather than His. When we try to be omniscient (all-knowing) and omnipotent (all-powerful), to see into and control what is to come, we place ourselves in conflict with God. In effect, we are trying to usurp His power in seeking to control what only God can control: the future. Our reality is uncertainty. The result of our refusal to tolerate this, by trusting ourselves instead of God, is that we become imprisoned by anxiety – fear. When we realise that our illusion of power is futile – we can't control the uncertainty – we become depressed.

Conversely, when we put our trust in God by having faith in His love, goodness, power and strength, fear is driven out and worry becomes redundant. We can entrust the future to God's safekeeping. By becoming God-dependent instead of self-dependent we find an unshakeable inner peace.

> *The LORD is a refuge for the oppressed, a stronghold in times of trouble. Those who know your name trust in you, for you, LORD, have never forsaken those who seek you.*
>
> Psalm 9:9-10

Remember:

- Most of what we worry about will never happen, or is about things we can't change. Threat is usually imaginary, the result of anticipation rather than reality.
- Worry and anxiety are pointless. They don't alter a situation or achieve anything positive.
- Live in the now. We cannot change the past and we cannot control what hasn't happened yet.
- We have to accept uncertainty.
- Ask yourself, "Has worrying ever helped me?"
- God is in control. Trust Him. Our attempts to be in control don't work. Fear creates imaginary threats and we react to threat with fear. In this way we become trapped in a self-perpetuating cycle that drags us down into depression.

Despair

Mark's Gospel relates Jesus' healing of blind Bartimaeus (Mark 10:46-52). The scene takes place in Jericho which has one main road running through it to Jerusalem thirteen miles away. It is Passover, when all male Jews over the age of twelve are required to go to Jerusalem for the celebrations. So the road is packed with thousands of pilgrims – mostly on foot, some riding donkeys – and in the midst of the crowds are Jesus and his disciples. But Bartimaeus isn't part of this flow of human life. He's hit rock bottom. Blind, destitute, no longer moving, just sitting in the gutter covered in a filthy cloak, he's given up. Life is literally passing him by. This is a vivid depiction of despair: someone who has just about lost hope.

When you're in the pit of depression, like Bartimaeus you want to withdraw from life, sit on the sidelines and let it flow on by. Retreating into yourself, you develop a 'carapace' that shuts others out, or at least keeps them at arm's length. Because you don't want to be with other people. You aren't interested in them and their problems; the demands they make of you; their cutting criticism and judgment.

Life now is miserable; the future bleak and frightening. All hope, joy and pleasure are long gone, never to return. The writer of Ecclesiastes encapsulates despair thus:

> *So I hated life ... All of it is meaningless, a chasing after the wind.*
>
> Ecclesiastes 2:17

Jesus is Calling You

CHAPTER SEVEN

Despair

How long must I wrestle with my thoughts and day after day have sorrow in my heart?

Psalm 13:2

Eaten up and worn down by our perceived failings. Lost in the past. Constantly replaying our shame and guilt, or living on our hatred and resentment of those we hold responsible for how we are now. Our future life appears doomed. Circumstances will not change and there is nothing to look forward to except death. As well as feeling hopeless, we feel helpless and powerless. We are unable to find meaning or fulfilment in life. Despair has taken control.

Feeling helpless and vulnerable is the result of living in the constant fear of anxiety. Fear stops us from *living* life because, as we've seen, it leads to avoidance behaviour. Submitting to fear in this way, instead of facing up to it, is self-reinforcing. Every time you give in to it, fear is becoming stronger and controlling you. Furthermore, this causes depression. Because when you surrender to fear, you feel even more powerless. You have a pervasive belief that you are at the mercy of a malevolent force that is stronger than you, that is in control of your life and destiny: bad luck, misfortune, fate, evil. When you think like this you know that happiness is for other people, not you.

But despair is an illusion. We create it by the belief that we should be in control of every situation, including other people's behaviour. When we aren't, which is inevitably the case, we feel helpless. In depression we ruminate on this, feeling downtrodden and powerless. This then becomes an habitual thought pattern leading to even deeper depression in which we identify ourselves as being a 'failure', believing that we are deficient and therefore cannot be successful. Our interior monologue and beliefs about ourselves are dominated by *shoulds* and *musts;* immovable, set-in-stone absolutes from which we will not waver. In the same vein we might make rules for ourselves concerning allowable behaviour, or pleasures and rewards that we will permit ourselves if we are successful in our efforts to control life: "If I achieve _____, then I can _____." When life is so uncompromising and you operate a system of personal reward and punishment based upon this, you are guaranteeing yourself a life of misery.

Why?

– Because perfectionism sets a high bar of attainment that is most often unrealistic; and then we blame and punish ourselves for being so 'useless'. Our despair thus arises from loss: frustrated goals of achievement; shattered hopes; loss of love (relationship breakdown, death of a loved one); loss of material wealth or possessions. Of course, these were all our fault, caused by our failure to manage life and be in control.

Helplessness leads to hopelessness. When you have such a negative view of yourself, believing that you are essentially flawed, you think that you can't change and life will always be wretched. This prediction of a fixed future is the product of an expectation of failure: you'll never achieve what you want. This, in turn, leads to feeling trapped, whereby you have no choices and there are no solutions to your problems. Thus you give up hope for change or improvement. You become immobile and inactive: "Why bother? It won't change anything." But when you're not moving you're not going anywhere. So how *can* anything change?

Eventually you come to believe that you are not worthy of love and care because, "I'm a failure." As a result you feel alienated and become isolated, deliberately closing yourself off from social interaction out of fear of rejection or any situation that could generate challenge or stress. Once again, fear leads to avoidance that serves only to exacerbate depression.

CHAPTER EIGHT

He's Calling You: Overcoming Despair

God's Healing Word

Take heart; rise, he is calling you.

Mark 10:49 (RSV)

We return to Bartimaeus, whom we left sitting by the roadside begging; a picture of despair. And yet, he still has a little grain of faith, as he senses that Jesus is someone who can help him (verse 47). He can help us too, however deep the pit of our despair and depression. When we hit rock bottom, what we are actually experiencing is a crisis of faith. The picture of blind Bartimaeus has much to teach us about how to overcome this.

Let's remind ourselves. What is faith?

– Having complete trust in God's love for you. Having confidence in His purpose. Relying upon His power and strength.

Figure 4: The path of faith

Just like Bartimaeus we may be crying to God, "Have mercy on me!" but there doesn't seem to be any answer. *I want to see! Renew my faith, restore my trust in you!* Still, there doesn't appear to be any help forthcoming. How quickly we forget how God has provided for us in the past! We seem to think that somehow this time is different and that He's abandoned us. But it is a provision that is available now and always, because in our darkest times God is still with us, guiding us, caring.

> *Even though I walk through the darkest valley, I will fear no evil, for you are with me...*
>
> Psalm 23:4

Essentially, there's a breakdown in communications. We are calling for help in our distress, whether we realise this or not, and God is calling to us, but we get so lost in the darkness of our problems that it's not easy to see or hear Him, is it?

The shepherd knows when one of his sheep is lost. Despite the crowds and the noise, Jesus hears Bartimaeus' cry. "He is calling you." When we believe in Jesus we become one of his sheep and he will lead us to all we need. After all, that is why he came; to reconnect humanity to God. How do we know that Jesus can meet our needs? Well, look at Bartimaeus! When we first saw him he was a hopeless case by the standards of the time, but his response to Jesus' call is immediate and joyful. He springs up, throws off that old cloak of depression and despair, and, reinvigorated, his faith and sight restored, he is transformed into a new man. This is the difference Jesus makes. Never doubt, we are secure in God's tender care; because His love is more powerful than the darkness, more powerful than our pain, despair and depression.

> *...the one who doubts is like a wave of the sea, blown and tossed by the wind.*
>
> James 1:6

The cause of our faith crisis (= despair) is doubt. We doubt His love for us; we can't see or understand His purpose; and we become self-reliant. In this way we stop focusing on God and fixate upon ourselves. Therefore, if we are to overcome despair, we need to refocus our faith.

The best, in fact the only, way to begin this process is in trust.

How do we know that God loves us?

– He tells us repeatedly throughout the Bible:

> *I have loved you with an everlasting love...*
>
> Jeremiah 31:3

This is a love that is not forgotten, abandoned or withdrawn; it is unfailing.

He shows us:

> *This is love: not that we loved God, but that he loved us and sent his Son as an atoning sacrifice for our sins.*
>
> 1 John 4:10

Such love is overwhelming and incontrovertible. There can be no greater love.

As Christians we know this, but in our despair we believe it is a love for others, not us. So wrong! Remember the leprosy-affected man in Mark 1 (see Chapter 2)? Look at Bartimaeus; roundly rebuked and scorned by those around him, but not by Jesus. No one is unworthy of His love and no one is beyond its reach, even you! In a state of depression, what we fail to recognise is that nothing can come between us and God's love.

> *For I am convinced that neither death nor life, neither angels nor demons, neither the present nor the future, nor any powers, neither height nor depth, nor anything else in all creation, will be able to separate us from the love of God that is in Christ Jesus our Lord.*
>
> Romans 8:38-39

You are not under the control of some malevolent power. It is our self-will, born of low self-esteem and self-punishment, which tries to block out His love.

When we are going through difficult times, experiencing problems, trauma or tragedy, we can't see God's purpose in it. When we look at the world around us riven by conflict and the apparent upsurge of evil, it is hard to understand where God is in all this. We have to learn to wait patiently upon the Lord. He has promised that He is working out His purpose (Isaiah 14:24), but not in ways that we can expect to comprehend and certainly not by our time frame.

> *"For my thoughts are not your thoughts, neither are your ways my ways," declares the LORD.*
>
> Isaiah 55:8

We can, however, be confident that God loves us, that all His works are perfect, and only His will can prevail because He is the God of all Creation. This is why becoming self-reliant is so futile. *God is in charge, not us!* When we trust and place our confidence in God, it naturally follows that we rely upon His omnipotence – His all-encompassing power and strength.

But if we doubt Him, we stop listening to His Word and listen to ourselves instead. Coming to rely on our own 'power', we soon find ourselves lost in a world of troubles.

Why?

– Because we are setting ourselves against God, trying to work against His purpose.

Paul is at pains to make this clear in his letter to the Corinthian church:

> *...so that your faith might not rest on human wisdom, but on God's power.*
>
> 1 Corinthians 2:5

He is God. Nothing can destroy or alter His purpose for our lives or for the world, (see Psalm 139).

> *...the testing of your faith produces perseverance.*
>
> James 1:3

Even when it feels like we are losing our faith, if we persist like Bartimaeus, who would not be silenced in his attempt to make contact with Jesus (Mark 10:47-8), if we continue praying, reading our Bibles, going to church, trusting in however small a way, God will reach out to us and repair that broken line of communication. Faith does need to be nurtured and cared for in this way in order to flourish.

It is only by having our faith tested that it can become stronger. Not everything in your life will work out the way you think it should. We have to accept this because it is not our will that prevails:

> *...all the days ordained for me were written in your book before one of them came to be.*
>
> Psalm 139:16

When you are going through bad times, take your troubles to God in prayer. Hang in there! God will help you and bring you through. Prayer is always answered. Remember, if you come near to God, He will come near to you. In this way, your relationship with Him will be made stronger and closer.

Hope springs from faith. Again, look at Bartimaeus. His seemingly doomed future with no possibility of change is totally counteracted and overturned by Jesus' call and his response to that call. We need to meet with God and open our minds to Him. God moves our souls to seek Him, seeking us. He reaches out, takes us by the hand and together we journey on. There is a constant flow of God's love for you. This is our dependable hope, and that's a promise!

> *...you lifted me out of the depths ... I called to you for help, and you healed me.*
>
> Psalm 30:1-2

Three Points to Cling To

- God will never let you down or fail you.
- Nothing is permanent. Predictions of an unchangeable, fixed future make no allowance for unexpected changes. After all, we live with uncertainty. Why can't this be good? Things pass. Change will happen.
- Stop focusing on present problems, past hurts and future worries. Are you going to allow yourself to be defined by these?

Jesus is Calling You

Uncomfortable Truths

We are all ungrateful and selfish. You may feel insulted or enraged by this statement. You might be quite sure that this does not apply to you. But ingratitude and self-centredness are two more features of depression that we need to face and address if we want to be healed.

In depression we focus only on complaint; how we feel, what is wrong with our lives, our many problems. This is, of course, entirely negative and results in our becoming insular and self-obsessed.

So much of our thinking is dominated by 'if onlys': "If only I didn't live in this place / house / relationship, I would be much happier," or, "If only I had _____ my life would be perfect."

Whilst we should all be striving to grow in spiritual maturity – becoming more loving, compassionate, kind, gentle, patient and forgiving – being constantly dissatisfied with our life sets us against God. Being out of sync with our Father, our Creator who knows us individually, necessarily means that we are imbalanced. Setting our will against God's, who is unassailable, is not only futile, but it places us on a collision course that can only end in our trouble and distress.

Jesus is Calling You

CHAPTER NINE

Ingratitude

For sighing has become my daily food; my groans pour out like water.

Job 3:24

Ingratitude is comprised of two elements: dissatisfaction and dwelling on perceived problems.

Dissatisfaction is pervasive in our society. Our focus is entirely taken up with what we want and feeling that we deserve to have more. You only have to look at a few popular newsstand magazines to see the truth of this. They are filled with articles that encourage dissatisfaction with your body, appearance, relationships and lifestyle. For example, "Get a Better Body"; "Look 10 Years Younger"; "The Way to Perfect Skin"; and perhaps 'best' of all, "How to Buy Happiness"![22]

The world tells us that happiness is to be found in wealth and possessions. Western society is *so* materialistic, more than ever before, that the simple but awesome pleasures of life have been either forgotten or belittled. The breathtaking beauty of a sunset; stopping to listen to birdsong; really looking at the intricate construction of a flower and savouring the intensity of its colour and scent; exchanging a smile or friendly word with someone we meet; gazing in wonder at the night sky; going for a walk with no other purpose than to feel the warmth of the sun, the chill of the wind; experiencing all of creation around us. And these are just a few of the things that *really* make life worth living.

---

[22] "How to Buy Happiness", Wired Magazine, May 2012

The world tells us that in order to be successful we must: own our own home and aspire to a larger one in a 'better' neighbourhood; be constantly engaged on our smartphones, tablets and laptops, upgrading to the latest model at regular intervals; seek promotion at work; and, above all, we must be young and attractive. We must have more, do more, want more. Bigger = better.

It is difficult not to be drawn into this way of thinking when you are surrounded by it from the Internet, print media, television, family and friends. However, the result of such a mindset is that we become acquisitive, constantly dissatisfied and therefore unhappy. We don't appreciate what we do have. Worse still, if we derive our self-worth from comparing ourselves and our lives to these world-given standards of 'happiness' and 'success' and find that we don't measure up, we can very easily slide into depression born of the belief that we are 'failures'.

The second feature of ingratitude is especially prevalent in depression – obsessive negative thoughts, whereby the whole of your thinking revolves around your problems and complaints, fears and anxieties. Just as physical illness and chronic pain demand our attention, so mental anguish can come to dominate our outlook to such an extent that we forget how much we actually have to be thankful for.

Thankfulness: Overcoming Ingratitude

God's Healing Word

Rejoice always, pray continually, give thanks in all circumstances; for this is God's will for you in Christ Jesus.
1 Thessalonians 5:16-18

Let's get to the heart of this issue of ingratitude. Why does it set us apart from and even against God? There is a very straightforward answer to this: because we aren't doing God's will. His will for us is that we should rejoice and give thanks at all times and in all circumstances. It's simple: being grateful and joyful brings happiness. The more you focus on the many blessings in your life, the less depressed – fearful, anxious, worried, blaming and despairing – you will be. When we become dominated by negative thinking it is because we are listening to the world, to human 'wisdom', instead of God. And when we listen to the will of man, we are quenching the work of the Holy Spirit. Love, joy, peace, patience, kindness, goodness, faithfulness, gentleness and self-control have a hard time flourishing within us when we are drowning in a well of self-pity. This is what separates us from the life of God.

We need to turn our will to being thankful, instead of dwelling on what we perceive as being wrong in our lives. So how do we go about doing this? First, we have to realise that our problems are not unique or unbearable.

> *No temptation has overtaken you that is not common to man. God is faithful, and he will not let you be tempted beyond your strength, but with the temptation will also provide the way of escape, that you may be able to endure it.*
>
> 1 Corinthians 10:13 (RSV)

Whatever we are going through, many others have gone through too and come out the other side. We are not alone in our troubles and we don't have to struggle on by ourselves. We can trust God to lead us through, if we will allow Him.

What is the "way of escape" that He provides us with?
– Faith.

> *The LORD your God is testing you to find out whether you love him with all your heart and with all your soul.*
>
> Deuteronomy 13:3

Do you?

REJOICE ALWAYS

Look for the positives in every situation. Viktor Frankl was interned in Nazi concentration camps between 1942 and 1945. In his book, "Man's Search for Meaning" (1946), he contended that whilst we cannot control what happens to us, we can choose the attitude we take towards events, ourselves and the conditions we face. In this way we can make meaning out of whatever circumstances we find ourselves in. There is always something we can be thankful for.

Try this exercise right now: think of five things for which you can be thankful. For example, a beautiful day, a book or poem you've enjoyed, a piece of music or song you've heard, friends, family, pets. When you really start thinking, you will find it is quite difficult to limit yourself to only five. This is a good habit to develop. Try it every day for a week and see the difference it makes to your outlook and, consequently, how you feel.

Let not your heart be troubled, neither let it be afraid.

John 14:27 (KJV)

But how can we be thankful when life is challenging, difficult and painful? Even then there are blessings if you look for them, not least those who care for us and about us; their love, encouragement and support.

In his book, "Miracle on the River Kwai", Ernest Gordon tells the true World War 2 story of an Australian prisoner-of-war about to be executed in a Japanese prison camp.

> *On the morning set for his execution he marched cheerfully between his guards ... Calmly, he surveyed his executioners. He knelt down and drew a small copy of the New Testament from a pocket ... He finished reading ... looked up, and saw the distressed face of his chaplain. He smiled, waved to him, and called out, "Cheer up, Padre, it isn't as bad as all that. I'll be all right." [23]*

How could he be so calm and cheerful?

– He'd been reading John 14:27: "Peace I leave with you; my peace I give you. I do not give to you as the world gives. Do not let your hearts be troubled and do not be afraid."

Whatever problems we might be experiencing are placed into stark perspective by this soldier's attitude when facing his imminent death. You see, he knew that he was not alone and that all would be well because he was held firm in the Father's care; just as we all are.

Whilst this is admittedly an extreme example of positivity, I am convinced that everything that happens to us is a gift from God. He is working His purpose out. Our life events, even the tragedies and traumas, can empower us if we allow them to.

How?

– By taking them to God for healing; asking for His help. When we are delivered, as we surely will be, we can then share our experience with others to enable their healing too.

---

[23] Gordon, Ernest, "Miracle On The River Kwai", (W.M. Collins Sons & Co. Ltd., 1963), p.89-90

*Every good and perfect gift is from above, coming down
from the Father of the heavenly lights, who does not change
like shifting shadows.*

James 1:17

We must resist judging and regarding God in human terms. He does not change His mind. He does not lie. When He speaks, powerful things happen. Nothing can prevent His will from being fulfilled. We can have total trust in His reliability and goodness. Your faith will become ever stronger when you submit yourself entirely to Him, admitting Him as your only refuge and anchor. Don't forget God's past provision and faithfulness to you; it is your promise of future safekeeping.

PRAY CONTINUALLY

God's Word never fails to uplift, support, advise and guide. When you're struggling with life, turn to your Bible; it is your prescription for living. It is amazing how many people who describe themselves as Christians don't do this! *Apart from God we can do nothing (John 15:5).* Look through the New Testament and you will see that Jesus continually gives thanks to God and prays before taking action, making a decision, healing. Note how thankfulness and prayerfulness go hand-in-hand. Do our prayers just boil down to making demands of God; always asking instead of giving thanks for what we have received?

And why did Jesus pray always? Why must we too?

– Because, along with reading the Scriptures, this is how we maintain a close relationship with God. It is how we can ensure that we are following His will rather than our own.

We have the sure and certain hope that prayer is answered:

*This is the confidence we have in approaching God: that if
we ask anything according to his will, he hears us.*

1 John 5:14

God heals, but He will *only* provide what we need to fulfil His purpose for us.

Being prayer-minded changes your perspective. I now begin my own prayers by thinking of the things from each day that I can be thankful for: what I've seen and done; the flowers growing in my garden; my family and friends... In this way prayer is focused on praise and gratitude instead of complaint and despondency. After a little while you find that this way of praying gives you a more joyful and positive outlook on life. By keeping your mind on God's grace, His unconditional love for you, you are listening to His voice, His wisdom, not yours.

When you are feeling depressed or experiencing problems and difficulties, take it to God. When you pray about your troubles, rather than relying on self-help, you are giving power and control back to God where they belong. Instead of becoming lost in self-pity and dead-end circular thinking, you are actively engaging with what is troubling you by opening your mind up to a spiritual perspective in place of a world-centred one.

Do you set pre-conditions, certain things must happen in order for your life to be improved? Are you waiting for life to turn out the way you think it should? Stop waiting; start living! Be grateful for what you have and experience today.

CHAPTER TEN

Selfishness

In his pride the wicked man does not seek him; in all his thoughts there is no room for God.

Psalm 10:4

We are obsessed with being happy. The huge number of websites on this subject, a whole area of psychological research (Positive Psychology), the growing number of wellbeing magazines and the whole focus of advertising stand testament to this. As a society we believe that we have a right to be happy. This is even enshrined in the United States Declaration of Independence: "Life, Liberty and the pursuit of Happiness". Largely what we mean by happiness is personal contentment and comfort derived from being successful, wealthy, proud and satisfied. Of course it follows that if we have a right to happiness, others have a duty to make us happy. So if we are unhappy we acquire a victim status; someone who has been harmed or injured by misfortune or ill-treatment. Thus, our ways encourage selfishness. We are excessively concerned with ourselves – our welfare, pleasure and self-gratification.

It is against this backdrop that we need to view our depression because we are all immersed in this self-centred society. In depression our focus is exclusively upon ourselves. We become totally preoccupied with how bad we feel; how terrible our life is, and blaming those we hold responsible, including ourselves; our feelings of shame, guilt, anger and hatred, worry and anxiety, fear, despair and self-pity; endlessly complaining about our many aches and pains, real or imagined, to anyone who will listen. It's all about *poor me, I am a victim.* Yes, this is an uncomfortable truth to face. I came to the realisation that my own depression was largely rooted in such attention-seeking. We want sympathy because it is pleasurable and gratifying; it makes us feel loved and significant. But attention-seeking has another element to it. When you are in pain it is evidence of an imbalance within the body. Pain demands your attention; it is hard to ignore and can overwhelm you. The emotional turmoil and mental anguish of depression is no different.

> *The mind governed by the flesh is hostile to God...*
>
> Romans 8:7

There can be no doubt that a self-centred way of thinking sets us apart from God. This is the sin of pride. If we are motivated solely by the satisfaction of our desire to be happy, our will ("the mind governed by the flesh"), we are not in a right relationship with God. As pain is symptomatic of a physical imbalance, so depression is the 'pain' we experience when we are out of balance with our Creator. Putting ourselves first leads to destruction because it goes against the greatest commandment:

> *Love the LORD your God with all your heart and with all your soul and with all your mind.*
>
> Matthew 22:37

The result of loving ourselves instead of God is that we become lost in a pit of despair; self-obsession causes our depression. Furthermore, because we are so wrapped up in ourselves and our 'problems', we become unaware and uncaring of others' needs, thereby contravening the second part of this commandment:

> *Love your neighbour as yourself.*
>
> Matthew 22:39

When we stop caring for each other there can be only one outcome: conflict and annihilation.

Love One Another: Overcoming Selfishness

God's Healing Word

Set your affection on things above, not on things on the earth.

Colossians 3:2 (KJV)

The antidote to our pride and selfishness is humility; thinking about ourselves less. The first element of this is turning our thoughts towards God. When our minds are on His commandments and precepts, when we look to Him for guidance through Scripture and prayer, this ensures that He is in control in our lives. His will is being done. In this way we can start to get back into a right relationship with God, back into balanced living. In a state of pride we cannot acknowledge that we are totally dependent upon our Father because all comes from, through and to Him (Romans 11:36). We must face the fact that there is no such thing as self-help. Look what a mess we end up in when we deny that God is in control. We need His help. Let God be God.

A further element of humility is brought out in the King James Version of Colossians 3:2: that we should *set our affection* on God. We need to love Him rather than ourselves, our 'wisdom' and human status symbols. We are corrupted by our desires, our will. Submitting our will to God's allows the Holy Spirit to develop and work within us. The first fruit of the Spirit is love. It is this which overcomes self-centredness.

Do not let any unwholesome talk come out of your mouths, but only what is helpful for building others up according to their needs, that it may benefit those who listen.

Ephesians 4:29

The attributes of love – compassion, kindness, humility, gentleness, patience and forgiveness – are all outward-looking; how we behave towards others. This is the third element of humility: fixing our minds on loving others instead of ourselves. Constant complaint and discontent does not build others up! Our bitterness, anger and ingratitude grieve the Holy Spirit and those close to us, and drag us down too! Conversely, when we allow love to flourish and grow within us, we can't help but radiate it out to others, through love's attributes, bringing them joy. Helping others brings us happiness too. You will find a new hope and passion for living in the fulfilment of serving others. This is our real purpose in life.

Do you have a mental wish list of things you think you need in order to be happy: success, wealth, fame, power, physical attractiveness, romance? Are you waiting to be happy by seeking these things, working towards a more 'fulfilling' life? A study conducted by San Francisco State University in 2009 even claimed that "buying experiences, not possessions, leads to greater happiness"!

Do you want to know the real secret to happiness?

– Stop wanting to be happy!

That quiet sense of peace we all strive for is not to be found through enslavement to worldly values that speak only to the self. It can't be bought. It can't be worked for. In order to find real life, joy and fulfilment we have to lose ourselves: our ego, our pride. Stop living for yourself. Live for others.

CONCLUSION

Listen to Him!

God lives in us and his love is made complete in us.

1 John 4:12

At the beginning of this journey to understand how depression develops and the steps we can take to defeat it, Jesus invited us to learn from him (Matthew 11:29). What have we learned? Nothing less than how to overcome the world!

We have become aware that the impact of worldly thinking is insidious and pervasive. Without any consideration of what we are *actually* doing, we succumb to destructive, habitual thought patterns that result in depression. It's easy to allow despair to overwhelm us; to blame, worry, fear, to be ungrateful and self-obsessed. This is a much more comfortable path to take than engaging in forgiveness, trust, hope and gratitude, which requires the loss of self-interest. Christ *shows* us how to overcome the world. He's calling you out of selfishness into a life of love. Accept it. Live it. Be freed by it.

Accept the love that is yours. God is love and we are of God. We belong to Him. He forgives, heals and redeems us in love. Ask for His help in the secure knowledge that you will receive it:

He lifted me out of the slimy pit, out of the mud and mire;
he set my feet on a rock and gave me a firm place to stand.

Psalm 40:2

Live the love. Love the Lord your God with all your being – heart, soul and mind. Surrender yourself to Him. Don't block the Spirit by your selfish will. As God commanded the disciples to do (Mark 9:7),

67

listen to Jesus. He meets all situations with love. Blame is overcome by forgiveness. Worry, anxiety and fear melt away when we trust God. Despair cannot exist in the reality of faith. Be an expression of God's love, not the denial of it. As you receive the healing that love brings, pass it on. Share it in caring for and about others. This is how love is made complete in us.

Be freed by love from the demands of your selfish and destructive will that is keeping you separated from the life of God. Be released from the torture of your depression.

> *Peace I leave with you; my peace I give you. I do not give to you as the world gives. Do not let your hearts be troubled and do not be afraid.*
>
> John 14:27

Notes

For Further Study

Commentaries and Dictionary

- Barclay, William, William Barclay's Daily Study Bible, (St. Andrew Press, 1956; 2004)
- McGrath, Alister, NIV Bible Handbook, (Hodder & Stoughton, 2014)
- Porter, J.R., The New Illustrated Companion to The Bible, (Duncan Baird Publishers Ltd., 2003)
- An excellent Bible Dictionary can be found at *www.biblestudytools.com*

What Shall I Read Next?

OCD: Be Still and Know
P.A. Kennan
ISBN 978-1-910197-66-0

What is Obsessive Compulsive Disorder (OCD)? Why do some Christians struggle with anxiety? Can the Bible help with psychological disorders? How can we break free from fear?

P. A. Kennan herself struggled with the debilitating effects of OCD – until one day she found herself in a life-threatening situation, and discovered the key to her healing.

Kennan describes the biology of OCD, then guides the reader through the relevant emotional and spiritual issues, providing practical insight that can lead towards recovery. Helpful both for OCD sufferers and those who are trying to support them, this holistic guide provides a biblical, Christian perspective on current medical understanding.

Available from all good bookshops, as well as from the publisher:
www.onwardsandupwards.org/product/ocd-be-still-and-know